writing
your story
with God

NFL Encounters of the God Kind

Dallas Neil

2019 • ISBN: 9781695152823

Intro

Some days I feel like a statistic. And not the ones you like to read about.

Statistic #1
One in 1 million high school football players make it to the NFL. Oh yes. That's me.

Statistic #2
Studies show that professional athletes have divorce rates of up to 80% in their lifetime. Oh yes. That's me too. It's not my favorite stat.

My name is Dallas. I currently run health clubs and perform business consulting for a living. I have always been an inspired person. Motivation quotes, business ideas, hopes, dreams. That is my game. Adventure. That is my passion.

I am now married to the woman of my dreams, Christy. I have three beautiful daughters full of destiny. My parents have been dating since high school and married over 50 years.

I am the son of a self-employed orthodontist. My mother is sharp as a tack and could have done anything she wanted. She chose to take care of me and my sister, which was no easy task. She also managed the finances of the orthodontic business.

When I was no older than 12, I asked my dad about his profession. The one thing I remember about that conversation was what he said about family, "I am able to be at your sports events and coach because I am able to make my own schedule." From that day forward, I was determined that one day I too would be able to set my own schedule.

From the time I was in 7th grade I would make goals, write them on paper, and often stick them under my pillow. Over the next 10 years, each one of those goals would become a reality for me.

After high school, life was a whirlwind. My college football team won the I-AA national championship my freshman year. I went on to become a GTE Academic All- American, and ended up being the first player ever to enter the NFL with a Master's Degree in Business. It was like everything I touched was turning into gold. My dreams were coming true.

In the midst of all that favor, God touched me deeply when I was 22 years old.

I had thought for the longest time it was best to rely on myself, and that seemed like a good thing. Trusting an invisible God seemed weak. The most strength I have ever found has been in a life pursuing the Holy Spirit.

Everything I have ever craved (adventure, laying it all on the line, pure untwisted love) is exactly what I found in learning to listen to God's subtle voice, and using it to mature my faith and life.

People may think that winning a national championship or making it to the NFL was the greatest experience of my life. Although amazing and hilarious at times, finding that Jesus was the one, true, living God and experiencing God's presence far exceeded any other experience. It has been a journey that both of us (God and I) have been on together even when I thought He didn't exist or wasn't there at times.

I think everyone has a treasure inside of them and an amazing story that God is writing through them. That is my motivation to write and share. To see the fullness of God explode in every person's life. To remove every hindrance and help each of us make a straight path to Lord. Nothing should rob the joy God has intended for you.

Through these stories, I pray that God would speak to you personally about your own journey and inspire you to new levels of joy and adventure with Him.

Chapter 1

I was born in Great Falls, Montana, which can truly be described as Big Sky Country. Apart from a few scuffed knuckles along the way, my childhood was quite dreamy.

By contrast, I hear of the horrific things many have gone through in their childhood and are amazed at how resilient and "normal" they are.

What am I trying to say here?

At this moment, the most important factor is not where you have come from. It is not an indicator of where you are going.

Who decides where I am going next? It's a good question to ask. We look back on our past and we can see God's faithfulness, but we look forward and often we wrestle about what is next. Who are we really wrestling with? Our past? Ourselves? Our fear of the future? With God?

I know what the Bible says, Love the Lord God with all your heart, all your

mind, and all your soul. So the question in this arises ... in all this love I have for God and that he has for me, who decides what is next?
WE do.

Doesn't God who has known me from the beginning of time help form my next steps? The answer is yes.

But don't I have a choice in this all? The answer is yes.

This idea of "we" is the most beautiful concept. We see it plastered on inspirational quotes similar to this: "We before Me". Something inside each of us loves that idea. There is just something God put inside us that craves to be part of something greater than ourselves.

Well then, what are "we" going to do?

••••

Sometimes you just don't get a second chance to make a first impression.

I was a free agent walk-on with the Atlanta Falcons. They bring in 110 guys in the spring and by the time training camp is over they whittle down the roster to 53. Probably 30 or 40 of those roster spots are already spoken for by established veterans on the team, which leaves only a few spots for rookies to find their way into the NFL.

This was the first impression I made:

Although I was hired as both a punter and a tight end, during training camp, I was an H-Back. This means I am on offense and sometimes the quarterback will hand the ball off to me.

Well on this day, my first time with my pads on in NFL training camp, the ball was handed to me and I blew through the line untouched. You see, in training camp, they often just "tap" you on the hip instead of hitting you head-on. It's a way of limiting the amount of abuse your body takes.

I went busting through the line and headed towards the strong safety, Gerald McBurrows. He was coming full speed at me and my understanding was that we were doing the "tag" drill. He will just tap my hip on the way by. Nope. It was too late to react. He hit me so hard I flipped 180 degrees and landed flat on my back with the crowd moaning "ooooohhh".

Once the lights came back on (it was a sunny day so this is referring to my consciousness), Coach Dan Reeves was standing over me and these were his words that I will never forget. "Son, this is the NFL, you got to protect yourself. NFL is going to mean Not For Long if you keep taking hits like that."

Hence, the beginnings of my training camp nickname, "Rudy". In this case, I think it was just because the guys on the team started to feel bad for me. Day after day, I was getting absolutely pounded on with my undersized body. At that point, I was only 210 pounds going against guys that were 250 pounds or more. My position coach rarely even put me in on the plays, as I think he was concerned I might get seriously injured or embarrass him.

Needless to say, at this point, my hopes of making the team were just about zero. I was still punting the ball very well, but I had a solid veteran punter, Dan Strysinski, in front of me at that position. My only chance of making this NFL team was as a tight end / H Back.

Sidenote:
There is no excuse for giving up. It's a choice. That sounds harsh. If the light of the world is inside us, then giving up is not our character. Jesus never quit on us as he endured for our freedom. The pressures of quitting will only make us more determined if we allow them to. What if we have tried and failed? Fail again. And learn something about ourselves. The light bulb was not invented on the first try. And the patient endurance we gain from pushing into the pressures of life creates an unstoppable force to stomp on darkness (fear) everywhere we go. Win a few battles inside ourselves and we will get a big appetite for overcoming obstacles in life.

••••

Hit of the Day ... It gets worse.

I remember reading the Greenville, SC paper and seeing an article called Hit of the Day. Training camp for the Atlanta Falcons was in Greenville and each day the newspaper would highlight a crushing blow from training camp to show off the best players.

I was highlighted in the Greenville paper a few days in a row as part of the Hit of the Day column. My parents must have been so proud (sarcasm). I was the one on the receiving end of the hit. Day after day, I was taking a pounding. I remember sitting down in the locker room after practice hurting so bad. I was not sure if I could pull my pads off because of the pain. Chris Chandler, the Falcons quarterback at the time, walked by and patted me on the shoulder and said, "It's going to be ok". Gosh, even the players are noticing how pathetic my abilities are against these giants. I wanted to become invisible. At that moment, that was the lowest my self-esteem had been.

What was I here for? Maybe it is time for football to be done for me?

Sometimes, when we are totally out of options, that can be a good thing. Read on.

The team took a trip to Tokyo, Japan to play in a pre-season exhibition game against the Dallas Cowboys. We hopped on a double-decker jet and spent the next 12 hours or so on a direct flight to Japan. It was my first time on a jet that big, and I clearly remember a couple things.

The stewardess on the plane walked around with a fancy tray that seemed to have an unlimited supply of ice cream sandwiches stacked very neatly. I ate at least 7, but some guys must have put down closer to 20.

Each player received at least 2-3 seats to himself. We had room to stretch out and relax. As I walked to the front of the plane I noticed that the entire general management and front office was squeezed right next to each other. I loved being an NFL player, but the royalty-like treatment never felt quite right. I was a 22-year-old rookie and these guys and gals had been working their tails off for years.

Once we landed, the NFL exhibition game against the Dallas Cowboys was the next day. I realized at some point during our pre-game practice my position coach had absolutely no intention of playing me in the game. This was likely my only chance to show the coaches that I could play at this level. There was only one week away from the first round of cuts. At that point the roster reduces from 110 players down closer to the final 53. It became clear that I was on the cut list.

During the 2nd quarter of the game, the starting fullback sustained a concussion (one of many of his career) and was out for the rest of the game as a precaution. The backup fullback, a 2nd round draft pick the year before, was now in the game. Early in the 3rd quarter, he suffered a hamstring strain and had to leave the game. This was my shot. There were no other backups on the roster. I was the only one left that knew the fullback position.

Standing on the sidelines, in awe of the moment, I heard Head Coach Dan Reeves yell, "Put the back up in". My position coach responded, "we don't have a backup!".

WHAT!? My coach had so little confidence in me at the time, it was like I was invisible. I stood on the sidelines realizing that I had just flown all this way to be in the middle of an internationally televised NFL game as a spectator in a fancy uniform. Coach Reeves screamed again, "Well then, put Neil in!" My position coach looked right back at him and said, "You can't be serious." True story. I was standing right next to them...mildly humiliated. Coach Reeves looked at me, grabbed my facemask and said, "Get in there."

Standing in the huddle, the next play was called and by the time I got to the line, in my excitement, I had forgotten the play call. Improvising, I ran a short receiving route to the left-hand side and the quarterback liked what he saw and threw it my way. Into my hands went the ball, then a quick dodge of an oncoming tackler and I was headed 25 yards seeing the goal line in sight.

Even though I fell short, the sidelines erupted. The guy (me) that had been absolutely crushed in practice and for all practical purposes, and had no chance of making this NFL team, had a small victory.

Getting bigger, faster, stronger

"We want you to gain a pound of weight a week every week until you are 240 pounds", stated one of my coaches. I looked down at my 210 lb frame...you kidding me?

The coach continued, "You will weigh in every Friday and for every pound you are under your goal weight, it will be a penalty of $250 per pound out of your paycheck. In addition, if you miss your goal weight two weeks in a row, the penalty will double to $500 per pound." I nodded my head but inside I was thinking, "You can't be serious". He was serious as a cemetery.

Every Friday, right before my weigh-in you could find me drinking a gallon of orange juice or whatever tasted good at the time. I never stopped eating for more than a couple of hours. Peanut butter and jelly sandwiches a few extra times per day. Mac and Cheese at 10 PM at night. Lots of sleep. Whatever it took, I was not going to lose $1,000s out of my paycheck.

In all my time in the NFL being around

some of the most amazing freaks of nature, I never witnessed or even heard of one player using steroids. At the time I played, the testing was consistent and completely random so that no player could risk using steroids and getting away with it. I remember during the offseason one year, I was up in Montana and I got a call from the NFL drug testing team asking where I was. I said, "At a cabin in Montana." To my absolute shock, they got on a plane immediately and flew to where I was and asked me to "pee in a cup". I tried to convince them it was a waste of time to fly all the way up to Montana, but I was "randomly" selected somehow. I was impressed by how seriously the NFL took eliminating drugs from their sport. Good job NFL.

You may wonder ... did I gain the 30 lbs in time? I did. And to my absolute shock, my speed increased during the process. The strength coach realized that my frame could handle a lot more muscle and that is exactly what he put on me, a lot more muscle. It also helped that during that time I was training with Olympic sprinting coaches. In the back of my mind, I knew if I didn't grow into an NFL sized specimen, the crushing blows of the sport would have no mercy on me. No more "Hit of the Day" for me. At 240 pounds, I was now a force to be reckoned with.

Chapter 2

What do Jesus and football have to do with each other?

The peace that passes all understanding.

I remember in college I was about 22 years old and I was freshly excited about reading my Bible, but I had no idea what I was doing.

Before one of my football games, I was lying on the floor near the locker room. I liked to listen to classical music sometimes to calm me down before going out in front of over 20,000 screaming fans. If I got too hyped up, I would run out of energy during the game.

From grade school and on, internally I struggled with a fear of failure. It was not obvious to anyone because I masked it with a high level of confidence in my natural athletic abilities. What no one probably knew about me was that fear of failing drove me. Although it sounds like a good attribute, if you are going to be a football player, it was exhausting inside.

Whether it was fear of letting people down or fear of dropping a ball in front of thousands of people, it was a constant feeling that I "had not done enough". The internal joy was hard to find for more than a few minutes.

Accepting Jesus into my life when I was 22 had lifted an amazing weight off my shoulders, but the question clearly remained: What do Jesus and football have to do with each other?

I had no idea.

Laying on the cold locker room floor that day before the game I opened up my Bible and was reading through the pages and came across this scripture: Don't worry about anything, but in every situation, by prayer with thanksgiving, present your requests to God. And the peace of God, which transcends all understanding, will guard your hearts and minds in Christ Jesus.

At that point in my life, I felt like putting God to the test on this one. I read it, sat up, and said to the Lord, "Well, I am just going to believe that this is true and do my part by presenting to you my requests with thanksgiving. Lord, I am asking you if the Bible is real, would you do your part of giving me a peace that is beyond my under-standing." Boom, closed the book and ran out onto the field.

That day I started to get this warm peace all over my body that felt like the Lord was saying, "Its going to be all right, I am watching over you." I be-gan to no longer be afraid of being in front of thousands of people because it felt like it was just me and Jesus on the field. As long as we (me and Jesus) were on the same page, everything was going to work out just fine.

This revelation became a new real-ity that changed the course of my life. There was likely no way I could have handled the stress of NFL tryouts, where I was constantly over matched physically, if I did not have this inner confidence with Christ that everything was going to be just fine.

My roommate at NFL training camp noticed this and talked to me about it. After some of the worst and most bru-tal days, he would say to me, how do you seem so calm? Aren't you worried about things?

When I needed to settle down after a long day, I would just open up my Bible and read. It would just be me and Jesus having some time together. No, I am not crazy. This is what following Jesus is about. It's not about me. It's about us.

While my roommate would continually share with me how he felt like a failure, I felt like a champion. And for the record, I was playing far worse. My performance was no longer linked to my identity as a person. I was more than just a football player, I was born of the Spirit in Christ and learning how to fellowship with the Holy Spirit.

This reality was creating an almost invincible force around me because fear no longer had access. I knew I was loved more than I could imagine. When fear and chaos leave, all that remains is peace. Chaos and peace cannot co-exist. It has to be one or the other. By choosing to follow Jesus in my life and listening to the Holy Spirit, I was receiving peace that was unlike I have ever experienced. It worked. It was what I was looking for. This Bible and Holy Spirit thing was real. More real than everything else.

Take a moment to reflect:

There are pieces of these stories that are meant for you. What is God speaking to you right now?

_____

_____

_____

_____

_____

Take some time to write it down either on paper or digitally. His voice (whether heard or felt or seen in pictures in your mind) is present in those quiet moments.

Chapter 3

Free Meal Dallas Neil

One of the most enjoyable things about playing in the NFL is eating. Yes, eating. You have to eat to maintain your size and strength and it takes a lot of food. Eating usually involved a large group of players going out to a restaurant around Flowery Branch (the Atlanta Falcons training facility).

Let me explain. One typical NFL player who is hungry can easily order $100 of food on their own. Yes they can. And we did. So now, multiply that by 10 players or so and you have at least a $1000 bill wherever we went to eat.

How are we going to split the tab? Same way every time. The game is called "Credit Card Roulette".

How to play:
Put your credit card in a hat and have the waiter pick out one card at a time. The last credit card picked gets to pay the whole bill. Oh, it is so fun, unless you get stuck with the bill.

Three years in Atlanta with the Falcons football team. Hundreds of lunch and dinner bills with the players and never, not once, did I get stuck with the bill. Now maybe I forgot my wallet a time or two, but the nickname Free Meal Dallas Neil was gaining some momentum. NFL players typically would prefer nicknames like Crusher, IronHead, or something that sounds more like a superhero.

For me, I was fine with it. Free Meal Dallas Neil had a ring to it. Anything to get a good laugh from the guys. The job of playing in the NFL was so stressful most of the time, laughing was what kept us from killing each other.

In the midst. Sometimes we find we are in a season to "learn". For me, my second year in the NFL was spent on the practice squad. Being on the practice squad means that you don't get to play in any of the regular season games and you get paid about one third of your normal salary, which at that time was about $75,000 per year. It was clear the coaches thought I had potential, but I needed more time to develop my skills and the timing was not yet right for me to secure a starting position on the roster.

When we are in a season of learning, we can't waste time beating ourselves up over the mistakes we have made. We have to celebrate how we are growing and learning. It may be hard to do, but this perspective is so important. We are being prepared for something greater only if we are willing to recognize and humble ourselves to the moment.

Can you see a challenge you are facing over and over again?

God brings forth the same challenge in different ways until you truly conquer it. Sometimes it can feel like a recurring dream. Often, these challenges are in our character and in the way we relate to others.

God helps us learn through real situations that will build up our emotional muscles and fine-tune our supernatural decision-making (being led by the Spirit vs. solely by our emotions).

Take a moment to reflect. What are you learning in this season of life?

_____

_____

_____

_____

_____

Write it down either digitally or on paper.

Chapter 4

"Face" Your Fears

Have you ever wondered why people say "Face" your fears.

The image that I see is a picture of your face looking in the mirror. Our fear only looks real to us. Many others don't see it looming in us.

Fear seems to stir thoughts in our minds about how bad it will be if things don't go well. The fear of how others will perceive us...how you could disappoint those closest to us...this line of thinking can go on forever.

Fear often leads to trying to control. The thought process can be, "I don't want to fail so how can I control this situation to make sure the outcome I desire happens."

At this point, because fear is in the driver's seat and has been given license (from us) to think, speak and behave based upon these fears, we also have a constant, subtle manipulation on our hands. Fear will lead us to manipulate people to get what we want. Even if we think we are a good and healthy person, when we operate out of a fear mindset, the fruit of it is control and manipulation. The people who we interact with will eventually feel that. It is a survival technique we adopt at times to get through life and "do our best". It is not our best. It is not God's best for us.

Reflection:

What do you fear the most? List the things that come to mind.

_____

_____

_____

_____

_____

It all comes down to what I put my trust in: Myself or God. The conversation I was having with myself at this point went like this:

Say What? It feels more scary and fear-ful to trust an invisible God that I don't yet know very well than it would be to just let my own fears drive me. All this unknown? I don't like feeling like I am not in control of the outcome? I don't feel like I know God well enough to fully trust him? Feels like too much to risk.

Then this scripture comes to mind;

"Trust the Lord with all your heart and lean not on your own understanding. Acknowledge him in all ways and he will direct your paths." Proverbs 3:5

We can choose to continue to operate in fear and control, or we can plunge towards a life of deepening our faith. The conversation in my head contin-ued like this:

I really just want to achieve my goals and it seems God can help. What can get me to achieve my goals the fastest and be the most successful? Sure I be-lieve in Jesus, but in the same sense, someone has got to do this.

I would say for much of my life I

thought I had faithfulness, but really it was a trained discipline based upon achieving goals and the fear of those not coming to pass. If I was being deeply honest, fear of failure drove me to achieve goals more than faith .

It reflects real bravery and courage to address those fears within ourselves and come face to face with them. Allowing those fears to come to the surface rather than hiding them deep inside is what brings them to the light. Once again, fear and faith cannot co-exist. The God kind of love drives out fear.

Faith flies in the face of fear and crushes it. Those two ingredients, faith and fear, do not co-exist. If we exercise faith (the light), fear must go. When we turn on the lights in a room, the darkness is gone.

Although it sounds incredibly simple and almost fairy tale like (because there is not a list of things you have to do to earn it), a revelation of God's personal love for us creates a totally different mindset. Its a surrender of our own self to something so much greater. A force driven by pure love. We actually get free from ourselves and our own fears. Our path now directed by an invisible, yet ever-loving God. Faith fueled by this "God kind of love" is unstoppable. It is total freedom from fear.

Faith like this just carries a different belief system.

Some lies that you will need to let go of:

The only way to achieve my goals is to make it happen myself. (self-focused)

I have to control the situation to control my happiness. (self-focused)

If I give too much, I'm going to lose myself and be unhappy. (self-focused)

The things that you must start believing are:

The best way to achieve your true goals and have joy is to surrender them to God and let Him guide you. (We before me - both us and God)

You thrive when you are generous and

selfless. God is a rewarder to those that seek Him. We see Him work most in our humility. (We before me - both us and God)

Your greatest joy is in relationship with God and others. (We before me - both us and God)

This can be scary if you have never grown your faith in this way. Please hear me out on this. If we give only out of our own strength and striving, it will be elusive to ever find the joy we are truly looking for. There will only be moments of it rather than a continual flow.

Let's be honest, becoming less selfish does not feel good most of the time unless there is some greater vision we are going after. That greater vision gives us the endurance and discipline to keep going. Following God is not always a feel good program as we are building new "faith" muscles. Every good thing worth pursuing has a price.

Chapter 5

Inner Strength - Finding the Lion Inside

Where does inner strength come from? It comes from a trust that is willing to go deeper than the fear we face.

How do you find strength that is greater than our deepest fears? Get to know the deepest love we could ever find. Someone who knows our fears better than we do.

When I was 22, I read a book by Joshua McDowell called "More Than a Carpenter". I was seeking true peace in my life and in the process of reconciling who God was and whether I even believed in him. Was Jesus just some glorified historical figure, a magnificent cult leader, or was he what people said he was...God in the flesh?

There was one chapter in the book called "Who would die for a lie?". That chapter talked through the logic of the 12 disciples that were closest to Jesus and their eyewitness accounts in the gospels and through recorded secular history. When Jesus died on the cross, these disciples freaked out. Many of them, like Peter, confessed to people he did not even know Jesus. In fact, Judas, the one who betrayed him for some extra money, died in a field from regret when he committed suicide. When Jesus was crucified, these disciples knew Jesus was dead. Many of them witnessed it with their own eyes along with the people of the Roman empire.

So why die for a lie?

History confirms that of the 11 closest disciples of Jesus, 10 died horrible deaths later in their lives. They kept proclaiming that Jesus was raised from the dead on the 3rd day, that the Holy Spirit of Christ was dwelling in them, and that Jesus was truly God in the flesh. These men died speaking this truth on their own, not together, all over the world.

1. Peter was crucified.
2. James was killed by a sword.
3. Andrew was crucified.
4. Thomas was killed by a spear.
5. Phillip was crucified.
6. Matthew was killed by the sword.
7. James was crucified.

8. Thaddeus was killed by arrows.
9. Simon was crucified.
10. Bartholomew was crucified.
11. John, was exiled, and died a natural death. Wrote the book of John.

This was not some cult suicide mission. In my head, I could not reconcile why 10 men in history would allow themselves to be brutalized, beaten, and ultimately hung upside down on crosses all while secretly knowing it wasn't true? I could understand maybe a few of them being crazy enough to do that, but to find 10 men in history who were running scared after they saw Jesus die, to turn with boldness unlike any others in history, and proclaim that Jesus was alive for the rest of their lives. They proclaimed this not just for a day or two, but for years amongst unthinkable torture.

For these men (and their families) to endure the humiliation, beatings, and toil all for something that wasn't true. No way? Imagine it. They experienced something that gave them the strength to face unthinkable fears.

That sealed it for me. Its true. Its real.

These men conquered fears like no one else in history. The strength that they had is the kind of strength that I want for my life. That was the true inner strength I was looking for.

What now?

So at this point, I knew in my head the kind of strength I wanted, but I didn't necessarily know how to access it. I told no one that I believed Jesus was God. It was a secret I was keeping to myself until I sorted more of this out.

My roommate in college asked me to go to church one particular Sunday. I said, "No, I am good." He returned my rejection with, "I will buy you breakfast." I flipped 180 degrees and said, "Sure I will go."

While at church that day, the worship leader stopped service and said in front of the whole congregation that he felt like someone there at church that day was wanting to experience God, but had never taken that step of faith. Even bolder than that, he said he was going to wait to continue worship until that person stepped forth. He said it in a kind, gentle way but it was still radically bold.

I waited a minute or two and looked around. Inside, I was getting frustrated. I was selfishly saying to myself, "I came here simply so I could go get breakfast and now this is going to take forever." So clueless. Then something happened, I felt God's presence and his conviction prompting me that this was my time. Initially, I hesitated, thinking about what everyone else was going to think and even my own pride saying in my head, "this is what weak people do." Then it dawned on me, this is my opportunity to take a step of faith to find that inner strength I was looking for.

Once I chose to take that first step forward, the hunger inside me for something greater took over. I didn't care anymore what anyone thought. Even though I really had no idea what to do, I dropped to my knees and confessed in my heart that Jesus was Lord. I surrendered my life. Tears were running down my face.

What happened next is unexplainable. I literally felt this weight lift off my shoulders. It felt like a 1000 pound weight was lifted off me. I didn't think I was sinful (hadn't really thought about it much), but all these burdens started lifting off me. All I knew is I just met Jesus and he wanted nothing more than for me to be completely free inside.

Not everyone's story of having an encounter with Jesus is necessarily like the one I experienced. It doesn't need to be. God meets us all at the place where we find our need and faith in Him. It always looks different, but it is incredibly personal.

There is always an encounter and an experience with God waiting for us. We have a God that is intimate and personal. God does not leave us to wonder our whole life. When we allow the hunger or something more to build in our lives to a point of complete surrender, we shall find what we are looking for. It's all about you and God, the we before me.

Even as you watch a movie like The Lion King, the turning point for Simba to come back to fight for his family was him overcoming his fear within himself. It happened during an encounter he had with his Father in the Spirit as he was hungry for answers. From that point forward, the boldness overtook the fear and apathy of doing nothing. Encounters like this with Jesus produce the same result. Bold like a lion.

Have you reconciled who is in charge in your life? Where your inner strength is coming from? Yourself or God.

Let that settle in for a minute. We can say we know God or believe in Jesus and still try to take complete control of our life.

That is the paradox. Let go of control so we can live free of the fear that drives us. Trust your Father in Heaven. Give up our life so we can find it.

He is the author and the finisher of our faith.

Don't wait...open your hands and encounter...

Chapter 6

Dreams

Ever since 7th grade, I have been writing down my goals and dreams. I would write down what I hoped to accomplish in my life. For the longest time I would put that piece of paper inside my pillow case. As I rolled over at night, the crinkling of the paper would remind me of the dreams and goals I aspired to live one day.

Whether it was the law of attraction or just the absolute mercy of God, from 7th grade all the way through the time I was 30 years old, those dreams and goals came true...all of them.

I dreamed of being an All State Football player - happened.

I dreamed of being the student body president at my high school - happened.

I dreamed of going to the NFL - happened.

I dreamed of traveling the world

encouraging others - happened.

I dreamed of earning over a million dollars by the time I was 30 - happened.

Each of us are 80% more likely to accomplish our dreams and goals if we write them down.

No matter what your age, what are some goals and dreams still ahead of you?

If you are ready, write them down on a piece of paper. If you are not ready to write them down or feel stuck dreaming, read on...

Death kills and tries to steal dreams. During my thirties I went through a divorce. Divorce is death in a way. Death to a life you thought you would live. Death to your dreams and in many cases death to your children's dreams.

For years, my goals and dreams never made it to paper. The fear of writing down goals and then not seeing them come to pass was just too much to bear. It felt safer just to not write anything down.

Death and disappointment had some-how caused me to look differently at the future. Previously, I had looked at the future as a grand adventure that held so much hope and promise. Now, it seemed, I looked at the future with more of a fear and hesitation. What if my goals are not right? What if God has different plans for me? So I just stopped dreaming big. My basic goal was just hoping next year will be better than this year. I was waiting on God for the big moment that he would swoop in.

I had become more of a victim to my circumstances. How? By waiting for someone else to fix my problems ... mainly God.

Before in my life, if I wanted something to look different, I changed it. Before, if I wanted to explore something new, I would go explore. Yet, now, I walked around with such hesitancy about ev-erything. I guess I felt like I didn't want to make any more mistakes.

The great thing about adventuring with God and the Holy Spirit is he can liter-ally turn our mistakes into some of the greatest things about our life. Do we tell a child when they make a mistake as they are growing up, "That's it! Life is over! Stop trying!"? I hope we don't. We encourage them to grow and learn. To gain wisdom as they explore.

It's time to dream big again. It's time to explore where we haven't explored before. It's time to seek the impossible, believe for the supernatural, and crash through our fears into the unknown ahead. Be bold. Bold as a lion.

But what will people say? It will likely make those closest to us uncomfortable. Growing is uncomfortable. People like to see you the way they have always seen you. It helps keep the relationship predictable. But you are not made to be them. You know who you were made to be. What makes you light up inside? Let them be them. You be you. Celebrate them. Celebrate you. There is more than enough love to go around. There is no need to judge or even have an opinion about it. Just be you.

What is one bold step you can take today towards your big dreams?

Chapter 7

Rest - Uptime Creates Downtime

When I was in training camp with the Atlanta Falcons, most of the players were under extreme pressure and stress. 110 players were asked to try out for the team. During training camp, each week, players would get cut after some of the preseason games until the roster was cut down to 53 players. Each week it felt like every moment in practice was a make or break moment. One dropped ball at the wrong time could cost me my job and the implosion of a lifelong dream. For many players, making the team and the finances that come with it could mean a totally different life for both them and their extended families. The pressure these players put on themselves was intense. The subtle pressure their families put on them was off the charts.

My routine after practice was to go lay in my dorm room bed for a while to get some rest in between practices. I would just lay there and read the Bible. Often, it was more like the Bible was reading me. Sometimes I would fall asleep because I was so tired and beat up. Most of the time, I would just read and my soul would begin to be encouraged again. The gospels contain heroes of supernatural inner strength and peace. Just reading them caused my entire mind to be refreshed. It would take me away from the obsessive thoughts of worry and fear and into a deep faith that God was with me on this journey.

My roommate would say a lot, "Why do you seem like you are never stressed? Aren't you worried?". I really wasn't. The physical stress was overwhelming. At times I had internal bruising from the collisions I endured. But my soul was at peace. The Lord was my strength. I knew deep down that there was a plan in all this. I would just continue to do my best and my best was good enough. I was allowing God to love me and I was loving myself. Fear had lost the battle. It could not and did not control me. Love did.

My roommate was not the only one that noticed that something was different about me. The coaches did. Not only did they select me as the 53rd player on the roster that year, which was a major accomplishment for a non-drafted player, but during that season the head coach asked me to pray for the entire team before we headed out for one of our big regular season games. I think I made the team only partially for my athletic talent. I think the big reason I made the team was I had the ability to inspire others to play better.

I modeled a lack of fear against all odds that caused others to step up their game. At times, I was called "Rudy" by the media. Rudy was a walk-on football player at Notre Dame that amazingly made the team. He was an inspiration to many and there is a wonderful movie about him.

Even though I spent most of my time in the NFL on the practice squad and not on the field on game day, I know I made our team better. It gave me great joy to do so. I was never the one getting interviewed, but it never bothered me. Many days I was happy not to have the pressure of saying the right thing with 10 microphones in my face.

••••

Side Story

My definition of exhausted: The feeling of the soul based upon not enough uptime or downtime.

Uptime is time spent talking to the Lord and having a dialogue about what would be best for the current situation. It is the WE time. Uptime is humbling yourself and loving the Lord with all your heart and all your mind and all your soul. Almost everything can be an act of worship and admiration when your heart is set on things above.

Uptime helps us know our downtime. When we spend our days in uptime and communication with the Holy Spirit, we can simply ask him, "When should I be taking downtime? And what does it look like right now?"

The God of the Bible rested too and he knows us better than we know ourselves. God cares about every last hair on our head. Yet, we have to allow him to care for us and be humble enough to follow the wisdom and guidance He is sharing.

Example: I remember choosing to take on some new responsibilities at work. They were challenging, but I was excited as well. Within a week, I was exhausted. My mind and body felt like they had no downtime. Even when I was around others, I had a hard time shutting my mind off. Finally, I had to separate myself for 30 minutes for some dedicated "uptime".

My wife and I asked, "What are boundaries for these new responsibilities we have taken on?" The answer came quite clearly and we talked about it together. No checking emails or discussions about the project outside of 9 AM- 6 PM. For me that also meant only working on this project on Mondays and Tuesdays.

Within days, my energy started to return. I started to get perspective again. I became present again. The uptime created confidence in knowing my boundaries as to what was God's best wisdom for the situation. I still had to make good choices when the temptation to keep working on these things came up in my mind and conversation. That is my role in the WE. Just say "yes" to the boundaries God had given me. In addition, give no attention to other distractions.

••••

What are some of the boundaries for your situation to create the downtime? Take some uptime to sort it out.

Chapter 8

Getting Fired is Normal

Getting cut from the team in the NFL is a normal part of the business of being a football player. The average NFL player only lasts about 2 years in the NFL and will change teams at least a few times.

I always respected the way I got fired when I was with the Atlanta Falcons. Coach Dan Reeves called me into his office. Of course, they always ask you to bring your playbook. If you ever lose your playbook, it is a $15,000 fine or something crazy like that.

I walked into his office with my playbook. I knew what was coming. Coach Reeves said, "My job is to field the best 53 players for this team. You are not one of the best 53." Boom that was it. It was straight to the point and left no room for questioning. The way he delivered it helped me maintain a sober reality about the situation. It was never about him liking someone else better or some political move, it was his job to determine who could help them win the best for that season. Even though it hurt in the moment, long term it was an admirable moment.

I replied to Coach Reeves, "Do you think I should continue to pursue football?" He replied, "Yes, absolutely, I will make some calls and see what I can do." Within a few days, I was on a plane to New York for a tryout with the Jets. Immediately, they offered me a spot on their 110 roster and a chance to try out for the 53 man roster. I played great football when I was with the Jets, and even though I did not make the official roster, the care that I felt from the Falcons organization and Coach Reeves has never left me to this day.

If you don't try something out, you will never find out if it works. Even though I was afraid of failing many times, the thought of having "regrets" long term loomed greater than potential rejection I would face. I truly believe I have my parents to thank for this character trait. They provided such a stable family structure growing up that I was not worried about failing I knew they would be there for me if I ended up with nothing. A lot of people don't have that security. I think it does make a difference, and am very thankful for their consistency.

We are the hardest critic of ourselves. We put unrealistic expectations on ourselves. Some of these expectations we mistakenly put on ourselves and some we allow others to put on us. These expectations mold our minds into expecting that things should look a "certain" way by a "certain" time. Going down this path creates a system of us "playing God" in our lives. I am not talking about goal setting here. I am talking about the unsaid expectations we have around life and that it should look a "certain" way.

If you choose to live a life surrendered to Jesus and the trinity of the Bible, then get ready for a ride. Things will not look a "certain" way. The definition of a Christian life is being led by the Spirit. And the Spirit in the Bible is sometimes described as a wind. You know not where it comes from and where it goes. There is an order to the "wind" but at the same time it is hard to see the big picture of where it is coming from and where it is going. In a lot of ways that is what makes it so good. We don't want to be some robots walking around. We crave adventure and majesty.

The Bible says that "through much tribulation" do we enter the Kingdom of God. We are talking about the King-dom of God during this life, not going to heaven right now. This kingdom the bible speaks of is "righteousness, peace, and joy in the Holy Spirit".

How else could we live a life of joy and peace in complete uncertainty? We could not without the partnership with the Holy Spirit. The We.

Why in the world would we choose to live a life of uncertainty (led by the Spirit) vs. trying to make things certain (try to control it ourselves)?

1. Because there is a reality that Jesus is the real deal and when you come to terms with that, you are willing to lay down everything for that truth.
2. Certainty is a form of "control". God's kind of love is the opposite of control, it creates a freedom un-like any other. We become so free

from ourselves and our certainty that uncertainty creates a deep sense of peace within us that God puts in there through his Spirit.

No folks. I am not nuts. When you surrender your life to Jesus Christ, his Spirit comes on the scene inside you and if you allow it, takes the driver's seat. The Holy Spirit was sent by God to comfort, teach, and help you. Thank God, we are not alone in this world.

We no longer need to be manically led by our emotions, stubbornness, impulsive thoughts or fears. We can charge our Spirit to connect with the Holy Spirit and lead us. Contrary to many opinions, this is not becoming a drone to God. This is absolute freedom with God.

When you love someone so much you would lay down your life for them, nothing pleases both of you more than when you can fellowship about what's next, go on that journey together, and share the experience. It is what we crave in relationship. That closeness. That oneness. That mutual respect and admiration.

That is Jesus. That is being lead by His Spirit.

Dreaming:

Use the following pages to write down your dreams and place them in your pillow. When you hear that crumple, that is your reminder to dream your dreams, not your worries.

Made in the USA
San Bernardino, CA
10 November 2019

59688522R00033